MAKING THE WORLD SAFE FOR HYPOCRISY

A collection
of satirical drawings
and commentaries by
Edward Sorel

THE **SWALLOW PRESS** INC.

CHICAGO

First edition

Published by
The Swallow Press Incorporated
1139 South Wabash Avenue
Chicago, Illinois 60605

ISBN (CLOTHBOUND) 0-8040-0564-8
ISBN (PAPERBOUND) 0-8040-0565-6
LIBRARY OF CONGRESS CATALOG CARD NUMBER 79-189198

Acknowledgments
    To Kurt Weihs, who took time out from his painting and graphics to design this book;
    Neal B. Freeman, executive editor of King Features, who seldom agreed with my
    point of view but never asked me to change it; Robert Manning, editor of *Atlantic*,
    whose concern for excellence persists in this Age of Aquarius; and Marc Stone, former
    publisher of *Ramparts*, who encouraged me to collect these drawing into book form.

Table of Contents

Foreword

It is not often these days that political humor—whether in column or cartoon—makes us laugh. The times are too bitter, the humor even when it is good astringent rather than outright funny; in fact some of the best practitioners of the craft complain they find it impossible to ply their trade since the advent of Nixon, whose administration has moved steadily beyond the reach of satire.

But looking through this collection I found myself convulsed, shaken, wracked with deep, satisfactory, long-missed belly laughs.

Edward Sorel has this extraordinary ability to nose out some small news item and then leap wildly away with it for our pleasure. For example, "Tricia Nixon feels that Vice President Agnew's attacks on the news media have had a salutary effect: 'I'm a close watcher of newspapers and TV. I think they've taken a second look. You can't underestimate the power of fear. They're afraid if they don't shape up.'" And here she is, Little Miss Nix-It, merrily knitting next the guillotine. Look closer and you will see the pretty thing is knitting names into her scarf: Cronkite, Reasoner, Paley . . .

Sorel is master of the really good pun (J. Edgar: We Pry Harder. Dayan: I Was Only Following Marauders) and a systematic avoider of clichés: who would have thought of a stern, close-mouthed Martha Mitchell rigged out as a majestic Czarina?

Jokes aside, there is much beauty and an amazing diversity of technique in these cartoons. The Nixon Library, one of my favorites, comes through with the impressionistic effect of a Rex Whistler stage set design. There is a wonderful Zvetlana in a meticulously pretty Persian miniature. The "movie posters" (Cardinal Spellman pensively fingering a rifle over the caption "Pass the Lord and Praise the Ammunition") are . . . movie poster art, bold, garish, compelling. The line drawings are in the direct tradition of the master caricaturists: Max Beerbohm, Daumier, Spy; and like their work will doubtless endure far beyond the topical events that inspired them.

The question arises, why haven't we seen more of Sorel's cartoons? *Ramparts* readers will rediscover the Bestiary series in this volume (Max Lerner as The Common Boar, Bobby Kennedy as the Varying Hare), others will recognize the Spokesmen from *Esquire*—but Sorel's News Service, one of the sharpest and funniest contemporary political commentaries ever produced, is unknown to most of us. The reason: it proved to be far too rich fare for the queasy stomachs of newspaper editors. For a while the series was syndicated by King Features, and at its peak ran in 44 newspapers. "But every time I got a bit vicious," Mr. Sorel told me, "some newspaper would drop me." The syndication foundered on the cartoon of Nixon juggling skulls (page 40), after which the series was discontinued by half the newspapers that still subscribed for it. "At that point it seemed futile to continue," he said.

Given this gloomy history we are fortunate indeed that Swallow Press has made the art of Edward Sorel, with all its viciousness intact, available in the permanent form it deserves as a source of ongoing delight and amusement in this handsomely produced volume.

Jessica Mitford

SOREL'S NEWS SERVICE

In this weekly panel, syndicated by King Features, the artist was allowed complete editorial freedom. Unfortunately, however, newspaper editors also had complete freedom to cancel, which they did in increasing numbers. The feature ended after 14 months.

© King Features Syndicate, Inc., 1970

Great Theologians of the Western World: No. 2
LANDING ZONE BALDY, SOUTH VIETNAM—During his brief visit to Vietnam, Cardinal Cooke of New York, celebrating Mass at an American regimental base 27 miles south of Da Nang, assured his communicants: "You are friends of Christ by the fact that you come over here." *(January 1970)*

1

Reason in High Places
WASHINGTON—On the eve of this country's second moon landing, a deep theological rift has developed as a result of the first. "The greatest week in the history of the world since the Creation," exuded President Nixon. Reproved Rev. Billy Graham from the Baptist State Convention in North Carolina: "It's the greatest thing since Jesus Christ." *(November 1969)*

2

Great Ideas of Western Man: No. 2
LONDON—In a sermon distributed to British golf magazines, Billy Graham suggested that golf is a parable for the Christian life. He reminded his readers that stance is important, advised them to keep their eye on the ball and follow through. If these steps are followed, the evangelist promised golfers will be greeted at the clubhouse by "the greatest pro of all time, Jesus Christ." *(August 1970)*

3

Lord and Order

MONTREAT, N.C.—Billy Graham has thus far refrained from commenting on Administration pro-
posals for "preventive detention," but a clue to his thinking can be found in the current issue of *Decision,*
one of his house organs: "The Christian is going to be faced more and more with the need to maintain
the delicate balance of social change on the one hand, and the loyalty to his country and to the system
in which he was reared on the other. 'The powers that be,' the Bible says, 'are ordained of God' (Romans
13:1), and the Christian citizen is committed to uphold the law and order that is necessary for the
functioning of society. Therefore, the Christian must be deeply concerned that a small minority
element in society is out to destroy that order." *(February 1970)*

Little Miss Nix-It

WASHINGTON—Tricia Nixon feels that Vice President Agnew's attacks on the news media have had a salutary effect: "I'm a close watcher of newspapers and TV. I think they've taken a second look. You can't underestimate the power of fear. They're afraid if they don't shape up . . ." *(March 1970)*

La Cause Celebre

WASHINGTON—In his recent State of the Union message, President Nixon reminded Americans that: "The greatest privilege an individual can have is to serve in a cause bigger than himself." *(January 1970)*

4

The Laird Is My Shepherd

CHICAGO—Secretary of Defense Melvin R. Laird recently told a gathering of 500 Presbyterians that Christianity calls on men to be "dual servants of both God and of the people." Men in public service must strive to "re-fashion" society to conform to the Biblical commandment: "Thou shalt love thy neighbor as thyself." *(June 1970)*

Making the World Safe for Hypocrisy: No. 1

CHICAGO—Looking forward to the 1970's, Mayor Daley praised youth and cited Jesus and Lincoln as models for today's long-haired, bearded generation. As for plans for the next decade: "I would like to see a real program—not a program, but real action on the question of how we live as human beings, what we are doing to one another." *(January 1970)*

5

Bureaucrat of the Breakfast Table
WASHINGTON, D.C.— Henry Kissinger, chief White House adviser on national security affairs, recently told reporter Gerald Astor: "I can understand the anguish of the younger generation. They lack models, they have no heroes, they see no great purpose in the world. But conscientious objection is destructive of a society. The imperatives of the individual are always in conflict with the organization of society. Conscientious objection must be reserved for only the greatest moral issues, and Vietnam is not of this magnitude." *(October 1969)*

6

Great Ideas of Western Man: No. 1
WASHINGTON: "As I looked at that movie," said President Nixon after "Chisum" was shown for him, "I wondered why it is that the Westerns survive year after year . . . one of the reasons is perhaps, and this may be a square observation, the good guys come out ahead in the Westerns, the bad guys lose." *(August 1970)*

7

In Trusts We Trust
WASHINGTON—President Nixon, speaking informally at the White House, expressed the hope that more young Americans would find in religion an answer to today's "crisis of the spirit." He suggested that there is too much emphasis on the materialistic side of life among the nation's youth. Shortly thereafter the White House released an official accounting of the President's personal assets—$980,400, chiefly in real estate.   *(September 1969)*

8

With apologies to Quaker Oats and the Society of Friends

Pass the Lord and Praise the Ammunition
WASHINGTON—The Religious Heritage Foundation of America, Inc. has named Richard M. Nixon "Churchman of the Year." *(January 1970)*

9

Tricky Deck
WASHINGTON, D.C.—"I am going to call the turn, my competence is in the foreign field . . . It's my strong suit," Richard M. Nixon recently asserted. *(May 1970)*

The Collectivist Thought of Vice-Chairman Agnew
WASHINGTON—Speaking before the Governor's Conference, Vice President Agnew surprised many in the audience by his use of classical Stalinist rhetoric. He called on the governors "to withstand the criticism of the liberal community, who are presently so blinded by total dedication to individual freedom that they cannot see the steady erosion of collective freedom..." *(March 1970)*

I Am, Therefore I Think I Think

WASHINGTON—Spiro Agnew on Spiro Agnew: "I'm still fighting the idea of being a rather ill-equipped, fumbling, obtuse kind of person . . . it seems fashionable to make out Agnew to be some kind of goof . . . I've got an I.Q. of about 135 when it was last tested. I think that's pretty fair."

(November 1970)

12

Cat Gets George's Tongue
PRINCETON, N. J.—The Gallup Poll shows Vice President Agnew enjoying rising popularity, particularly in 13 Southern states. In a recent survey, Mr. Agnew's rating had climbed to 25 per cent "highly favorable" in the South. The poll has apparently caught the attention of George Wallace, former governor of Alabama, who accused the Nixon Administration of adopting most of his policies. Singling out Agnew, he said: "He's a copy cat. I said everything he's saying now first." *(December 1970)*

In Your Heart You Know He's Right
FORT LAUDERDALE, Fla.—Seeking the Republican nomination for senator, G. Harrold Carswell promised an audience that "whatever the present level of mediocrity is in the Senate today, it will be raised when Harrold Carswell is elected." *(August 1970)*

14

The Bard of Wall Street
NEW YORK—William Shakespeare got his comeuppance in a recent issue of Progressive Labor's newspaper, *Challenge*. "Romeo and Juliet may be about some people who lived a long time ago, but it's chock full of the kind of idealistic lies that help keep capitalism going today," the editors warn. "Whose side is the 'just and impartial' Prince really on? . . . If he was so concerned about the people of Verona, how come he never forced the lords to pay for all the produce they ruined in the marketplace?" *(May 1970)*

15

Great Theologians of the Western World: No. 1
MONTREAT, N. C.—Billy Graham has acknowledged that he no longer emphasizes the fire and brimstone aspect of hell as he once did, nor does he maintain that heaven is 1,600 miles in each direction. But he still asserts that heaven is an actual physical place, though not necessarily in *our* solar system. "Some people have speculated that it's the North Star," he ventured, "but this is all speculative." *(August 1969)*

16

The Wonderful World of Wilhelm II
NEW YORK—Reaffirming his opposition to the recognition of Red China, William F. Buckley Jr. recently opined to a magazine interviewer that "we are hardly ignoring a country by failing to recognize it. As a matter of fact, we are sort of super-recognizing it. The easy thing to do is to recognize; if you don't recognize, you're giving it very special attention." *(September 1970)*

17

Lord High Sexicutioner

NEW YORK—David Susskind, television's jack-of-all-tirades, is at it again: "I'm sick of the women's liberation bursting into the *Ladies Home Journal*, seizing the office . . . It wouldn't work with me at all. If they ever came around here, I'd throw them the hell out. I'd tell them, 'If I see you one more time, the women that are working here won't be working here. Understand? Get out of my hair! Don't bother me!' Yeah, I would really fire a girl. I'd give them one sacrificial offering. There's always one person around you don't want very much anyhow." *(September 1970)*

18

A Satisfied Cadaver Is Our Best Advertisement
PARIS—South African heart surgeon Christiaan Barnard, arriving with his bride at their suite in the Hotel George V, immediately began a series of interviews with the press. After several questions about Dr. Barnard's apparent desire for publicity, one reporter asked: "Do you think all that publicity has hurt your career?" The answer: "You've never heard any of my patients complaining about the way I'm treating them now, have you?" *(April 1970)*

Sock It to 'Em, Mao Baby
TOKYO—The top pop tune in Communist China is a new anti-Russian song called "Smash a New Czar." A correspondent for the Japanese Kyodo news agency reports that the song is played every day on radio stations around the country. Chinese ideologists often accuse the Russians of reverting to the repressive days of the Czar. *(November 1969)*

Tyrant for a Democratic Society
CAN THO, VIETNAM—President Nguyen van Thieu said his fondest wish is to take part in an anti-war demonstration in the United States. "I'm anti-war, too," said Thieu. "The thing the demonstrators seem to miss, however, is knowing the difference between who is waging the war and who is trying to defend democracy and freedom." *(April 1970)*

19

It's a Bird . . . It's a Plane . . . It's Superbotch
WASHINGTON—The F-111 will require overhauling 450 planes at an expected cost of $80 million. A Senate subcommittee also revealed that the F-111, which has cost more than three times the original estimate, is "seriously short in engineering power." But, says vice commander of the Air Force Systems Command John W. O'Neill: "The F-111 is a very good airplane." *(January 1970)*

All Still Quiet on the Eastern Front (or Campus Rhythm of 1984)
MOSCOW—Leonid Brezhnev contrasted the "stormy upsurge" of youth in the West with the calm in the Soviet Union saying that Soviet youth "is growing up morally healthy . . . for the cause of the party, for the cause of Communism." Earlier, Amnesty International, a British-based private organization, revealed that Soviet political dissenters are now forced into psychiatric hospitals. *(May 1970)*

20

from *New York* Magazine, 1968

Humpty Together Again
MINNEAPOLIS—Hubert H. Humphrey, ecstatic over his victory in the Minnesota Senatorial primary, said he felt "as if I had a whole new set of glands." The former vice president, once a staunch supporter of the war in Southeast Asia, has changed his mind about that conflict. "One thing's for sure," he said. "Nobody's going to be elected president by trying to win that stupid war." *(August 1970)*

Egg O' My Heart
ST. LOUIS—Hubert Humphrey to the *Post–Dispatch:* "I think President Nixon wants to get out. I would have been proceeding that way, but a little more carefully. We have to be careful not to let Thieu collapse." *(March, 1971)*

21

22

Power to the Puppet
MINNEAPOLIS—Speaking to a Democratic party study group, Hubert Humphrey said he disagreed with those who suggested doing away with party conventions in favor of a national presidential primary. While acknowledging the presence of a "circus atmosphere" in previous conventions, Mr. Humphrey emphasized that it is essential to erase "the impression that they are rigged." *(January 1970)*

La Paloma

Hawk Talker Becomes Dove Lover
NEW YORK—Although he staunchly defended President Johnson's Vietnam policies when he was Ambassador to the United Nations, gubernatorial candidate Arthur J. Goldberg says he now favors "prompt withdrawal of all American troops, including air and naval artillery units." *(April 1970)*

24

Rabbi Feller
NEW YORK—Although Gov. Nelson Rockefeller may spend up to $6 million in his campaign for re-election, he is concerned about losing the Jewish vote to his opponent, Arthur Goldberg, who is Jewish. In a recent interview, Rockefeller traced his family tree and said: "My ancestors may have been Jewish. We're really not sure." *(September 1970)*

25

The Voice Isn't All He Throws
NEW YORK—Governor Nelson Rockefeller, when asked by a reporter for his views on Vietnam "My position on Vietnam is very simple. I think that our concept as a nation, and that our actions, have not kept pace with the changing conditions. And therefore our actions are not completely relevant today to the realities of the magnitude and the complexity of the problems that we face in this conflict." Asked the reporter, "What does that mean?" Replied the Governor, "Just what I said." *(September 1969)*

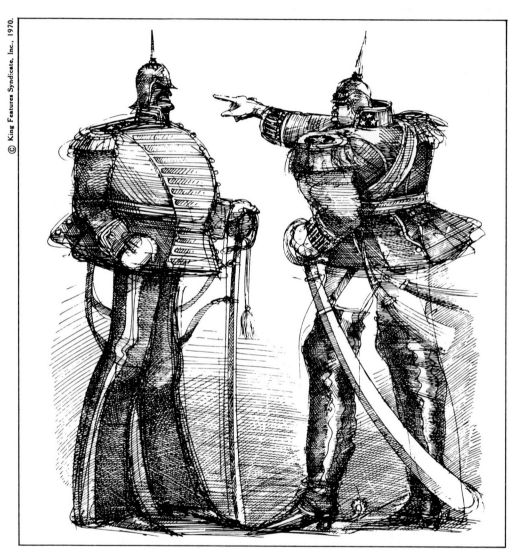

'Doves' Find Themselves in Hawkward Position
NEW YORK—Seeking re-election to a fourth term, Governor Nelson Rockefeller has accused his opponent, Arthur Goldberg, of "having acted as world spokesman for President Johnson's war policy for three years." Mr. Goldberg, for his part, has attacked Rockefeller's "long-standing and unswerving support of this war and its escalation." Both men see themselves as "peace candidates." *(July 1970)*

Smile! You're on Candid Camera

WASHINGTON—The weekly newsletter *Hard Times* last week carried an exclusive on Martha Mitchell, wife of the Attorney General. Their story stated that after attending a party at the Israeli Embassy and settling into her limousine, Mrs. Mitchell sighed to her companion Mrs. Gilbert Hahn: "I'm sure glad to get away from all these Jews." Mrs. Hahn, wife of the chairman of the Washington, D.C. City Council, is Jewish. *(unpublished)*

Gall in the Saddle

SACRAMENTO—Maureen Reagan, daughter of Ronald Reagan, recently returned from a USO tour of Vietnam. An advocate of military victory before her visit, she now favors a negotiated settlement. Reacted her father the governor (a former USO entertainer): "While I'm partial to my daughter and love her very much, I don't think foreign policy should be decided by USO entertainers." *(March 1970)*

28

Kettle Calls Pot Anti-Black
WASHINGTON—George Meany, president of the A.F.L.-C.I.O., defender of the exclusionist policies toward Negroes practiced by many building trades unions, branded the nomination of Judge G. Harrold Carswell to the Supreme Court as "a slap in the face to the nation's Negro citizens." *(February 1970)*

29

Making the World Safe for Hypocrisy: No. 2
SAIGON—Ambassador Ellsworth Bunker, ignoring the fact that the United States has dropped more bombs on Vietnam (North and South) than on the Axis powers during World War II, assured his audience in a recent speech that "we are engaged in fighting a limited war, for limited objectives with limited resources." *(April 1970)*

30

I Am an American
HOLLYWOOD—In an interview, John Wayne condemned the "yella bastards in the country who would like to call patriotism old-fashioned." He also explained why he decided to join up during World War II: "I would have had to go in as a private. I took a dim view of that." *(July 1970)*

31

Malice in Wonderland

ALGIERS—Despite promises to return to the U.S. where he faces prison, Eldridge Cleaver remains in this Arab capital, writing and giving interviews. He recently told an American newsman: "The goal is to take Senator McClellan's head. Now the process of getting his head has to rely on a strategic technique. I mean I won't just walk in and take his head and walk out, you see. I have to get past the guards . . . that would mean shooting my way in and shooting my way out . . . This is not rhetoric. I am telling you that Richard M. Nixon, J. Edgar Hoover, Senator McClellan etal . . . have to be apprehended . . . the fate they receive would depend upon the resistance they put up." *(February 1970)*

32

Dodd Works in Mysterious Ways
HARTFORD—Senator Thomas J. Dodd of Connecticut, who was censured by the Senate for diverting political funds to his private use, has announced his candidacy for a third term. Senator Dodd declared that his campaign for re-election to the Senate "will be based on my record of more than 15 years in the Congress of the United States. That record is an open book." *(March 1970)*

Caution: Foreign Aid May Be Hazardous to Your Health
WASHINGTON—In spite of the Administration's well-publicized drive against narcotics, the White House last week approved a $40 million development loan to Turkey, the country that supplies about 80 per cent of the heroin smuggled into the United States. *(June 1970)*

On a Kleindienst You Can See Forever
PHOENIX, Arizona—Deputy Attorney General Richard G. Kliendienst told a group of Arizona businessmen in 1969: "While Richard Nixon is President, random civil disorder will not be seen in America." *(August 1970)*

33

The Silenced Americans
HOUSTON, Texas—Radio station KPFT-FM has been bombed off the air for the second time this year. Broadcasters have urged federal investigation of the dynamite bombings, the office of Attorney General Mitchell has not acted. The station, disappointed, claims not to be surprised since its management is anti-war and pro-civil rights. *(November 1970)*

A Czar Is Born
WASHINGTON—Mrs. Mitchell on November's Washington anti-war demonstration: "I don't think the average Americans realize how desperate it is when a group of demonstrators, not peaceful demonstrators, but the very liberal Communists, moved into Washington . . . my husband made the comment to me, looking out the Justice Department it looked like the Russian revolution going on." *(December 1969)*

34

Ladies and Gentlemen . . . the President of the United States
SAIGON—United States headquarters reported that 65 Americans had been killed in Vietnam during the first week in September. This brought to 43,568 the number of Americans killed in Indochina fighting since Jan. 1, 1961. Meanwhile, in Washington, President Nixon gave his definition of fun: "Fun is the opportunity to do things you couldn't do if you were not President." *(October 1970)*

35

My Life at Hamdom House (or Getting Beneath the Cerface)
NEW YORK—Asked why he lends his name to a hard-sell mail-order business like the Famous Writers School, Bennett Cerf replied: "Frankly, if you must know, I'm an awful ham—I love to see my name in the papers!"

36

Saint Clemens

AUSTIN, Tex.—Mark Twain, dead for 60 years, appears slated to become "the saint of human laughter" through the offices of Mrs. Madalyn Murray O'Hair, self-proclaimed bishop in her newly-founded religion. In citing Twain's qualifications for sainthood, Mrs. O'Hair, who won a Supreme Court ban on public school prayer, noted that Twain "incidentally was an atheist."

Sorel's Film Festival

From *New York* magazine, 1970

This year's new releases—an embarrassment of riches—made the selection of films for our first annual festival unusually difficult. Not included, but worthy of praise, were *Gidget Gets Married,* starring Trish Nixon; *Pubic Enemy,* with Irving Kristol; *What Price Glory?* co-starring Andrew Sarris and John Simon; and *The Secret Sharer,* which introduces the exciting newcomer Daniel Ellsberg. Ed Sorel, artist and cinéaste, has drawn the posters and written the copy for these winners.

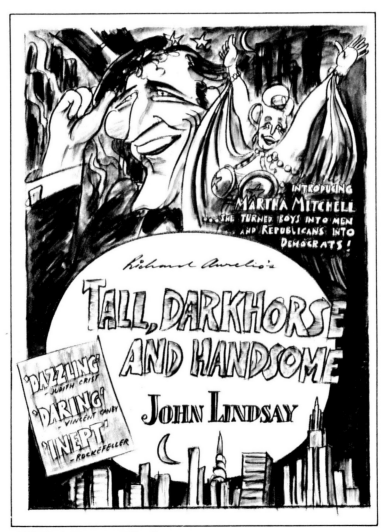

Tall, Dark Horse, and Handsome

After an absence of almost three days, John Lindsay returns to the screen in this year's brightest urban comedy. The plot is familiar but loaded with twists. A handsome, ambitious orifice seeker suddenly realizes there are no openings. He angers the wife of an attorney general and decides to seek asylum elsewhere. Dressed in white robes and riding a donkey he leaves home and proclaims himself the Messiah. There's a surprise ending no one will be seated in the last five months of the '72 campaign.

38

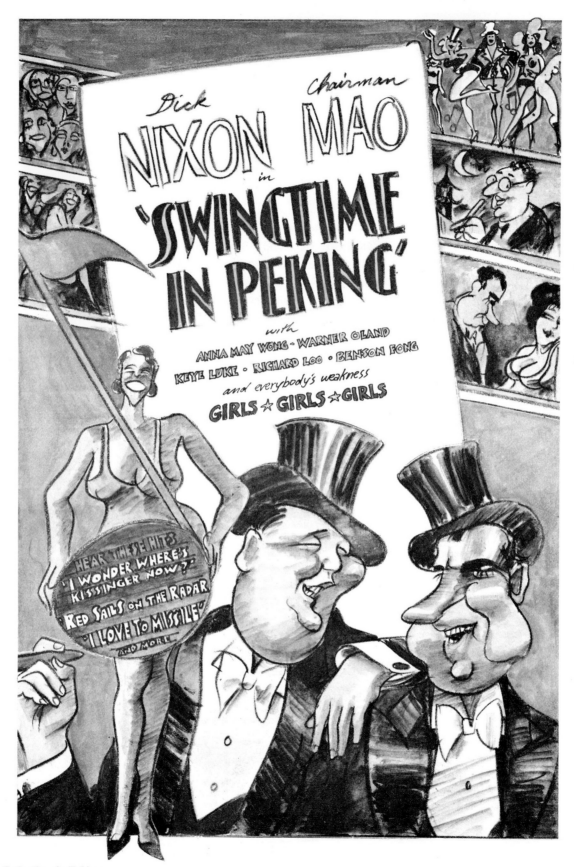

Swingtime in Peking

This year's smash hit (even before it opens) is a comedy adventure musical whose plot turns on a case of mistaken identity. The fun begins in an unnamed have-not country in the West when a droll absent-minded professor, played by Henry Kissinger, loses his glasses and is mistaken for a wise foreign policy adviser, played by Bill Rogers, who is miscast. The country's president, played—to the hilt—by Dick Nixon, needs glasses, is too vain to wear them, but joins in the search for the professor's glasses anyway. In a hilarious hunt, Dick and Henry wander all over Southeast Asia, making friends. They wind up exchanging toasts with Chairman Mao in Peking, where Dick sings the hit song *I've Grown Accustomed to His Race*.

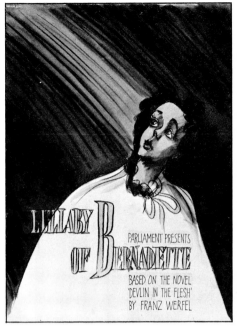

The Peaceniks Strike at Dawn

Johnny Mitchell, another bright discovery of director Richard Milhous and his comedy workshop, makes a strong bid for stardom in this exciting, big-budget Western. Tired of being just a dashing Wall Street lawyer with Robin Hood impulses (he takes from the poor and gives to the rich), John decides to go out West and take a job as sheriff. Uncertain who the real criminals are, he rounds up the entire town and jails everyone who isn't wearing an American flag in his lapel. The town is grateful.

Lullabye of Bernadette

The true story of Bernadette of Dublin, a poor but virtuous member of Parliament. One day a winged messenger from an unnamed supernatural power visits her and tells her that she will give birth to a son, who shall be a hero unto the working class. Delighted at the news, she gives the press a prepared statement and then gives birth to a daughter, which restores her faith in clods and encourages her to run for reelection. Flawed but powerful, the film rebukes those who say, "They don't make miracles the way they used to."

39

40

Atlantic magazine, 1969

41

First In War, First In Peace, First In the Heart of His Country Club

National Lampoon, 1971

42

Esquire magazine, 1968

"I'm not making a picture [*The Green Berets*] about Vietnam, I'm making a picture about good against bad. I happen to think that that's true about Vietnam, but even if it isn't as clear as all that, that's what you have to do to make a picture. It's all right, because we're in the business of selling tickets.

"It's the same thing as the Indians. Maybe we shouldn't have destroyed all those Indians, I don't know, but when you're making a picture, the Indians are the bad guys."

—*Mike Wayne, producer of* <u>The Green Berets</u>, *starring his father, John Wayne*

43

President de Gaulle was reported to have barred state payment for contraceptives on the ground that they were used for pleasure, not health. "Social Security has no more reason to pay for the pill than for automobiles. It is a diversion."

Local film producer contacted Richard Burton for a picture which (he hopes) could costar Burton and Liz Taylor.
Actor replied, "I'll examine the script, of course—but I wish you chaps could get it into your heads that we have done five films together—but that does not make us Laurel & Hardy."
—Variety

Redbook, 1969

46

Esquire, 1968

New York magazine, 1968

"We're looking for people who want to write."

50

Re: Famous Artist's School

Possible But Unlikely

Predictions made in '70 and '71 that somehow never materialized

New York magazine, 1970

While campaigning, Arthur Goldberg proudly reminds his audience of his role as UN Ambassador under Johnson.

51

Norman Vincent Peale tells his congregation to divest themselves of their worldly goods

National Lampoon, 1971

J. Edgar Hoover and Randy Agnew are discovered together in a motel.

New York magazine, 1970

Sammy Davis Jr. tries to get through a TV talk show without reminding everyone he is black, a Jew, and blind in one eye.

Mrs. Onassis gets a set of Teflonware for her anniversary.

New York magazine, 1970

Bert Parks attempts to kiss Miss America and discovers she's from Women's Liberation.

The Attorney General and Mrs. Mitchell have the Thurgood Marshalls over for dinner.

Bennett Cerf
stays up all night correcting
student papers from
The Famous Writers School.

National Lampoon, 1971

54

THIS IS A WALL STREET IMPERIALIST. HE IS GOING TO WASHINGTON. HE IS GOING TO DEMAND AN END TO THE WAR.

THIS IS A HERO OF THE WORKING CLASS. HE IS GOING TO WALL STREET. HE IS GOING TO SLUG STUDENTS WHO DEMAND AN END TO THE WAR.

THIS IS A NOTED SOVIET "AMERICA WATCHER". HE LIVES IN MOSCOW. HE IS GOING TO HAVE A NERVOUS BREAKDOWN.

55

Edward Sorel

The Bestiary

From the series in *Ramparts* magazine, 1965-66.

"There is nothing wicked about being the party of business."

The Jackal

(Lox Vox)

Scarcely any animal is less understood or more confusedly described than this voracious little beast. Conservative naturalists observe with satisfaction that his fur rises at the mention of a stock transfer tax, while liberal naturalists note only that the fur has a union label. (This may serve to explain why the Jackal is referred to as *Jake* on Wall Street and *Jackalla* on the lower east side.)

The female of the species has an apparent aversion to the damp intellectual climate along the Potomac in which her mate thrives. This causes a problem which is solved only on weekends when the male migrates north. This ritual may end, however, if he succeeds in becoming the number two beast of the jungle. This is unlikely, as the *Thespis Californicus* from the west (see *Bestiary*, October, 1966) certainly tries harder.

The Jackal, despite the unpleasant characteristics common to all vote scavengers, is not without friends in the jungle. Blackbirds like him for the way he uses his sharp clauses in their behalf; Hawks, for his participation in their pro-war "patriots parade" down Fifth Avenue. The Grand Old Elephant is less impressed, and keeps him in his place, while the Doves see him not as *Jackal* but as *Hyde*.

"In religion alone lies the hope for lasting peace."

The Cardinal
[*Spellmanus Bellicosus*]

The most familiar tufted redbird in the Western hemisphere, he is easily recognized by his tilted head, smiling beak and benign expression. His eyes are usually turned heavenward, in anticipation of enemy aircraft. Although possessed of a pentagon-like wanderlust, his customary nesting place is in the sparsely wooded canyons of Madison Avenue. In the fall, when his flock swoops to the polls, all species of Kingfish pay him homage but it is Tammany Warblers that the Cardinal takes under his wing. In his periodic migrations to the feeding stations along the Potomac he is always welcomed by the local Hawks who enjoy hearing him sing the praises of Franco-birds, McCarthy-birds and Diem-birds. Recent climatic changes along the Tiber have not affected his cold warble and he still migrates there from time to time to entertain Vatican bird-watchers with his lovely whistling of "Stars and Stripes Forever." The march of the doves, a recent phenomenon, has a negative effect upon him and he ruffles his feathers at the sight. Out-of-tune fledglings must become listeners or suffer banishment to some remote South American aviary. So too, those unfortunate novices who fly out of line with his right-wing formation. Although the Cardinal sanctuary is governed by local ordinances (separation of perch and state), this bird of pray does not suffer rules gladly.

58

The Parrot
[*Goldbergus platytudinus*]

Above we see the Pale-headed Broadtail (or Talltale as he is sometimes known), easily recognized by his thick-tufted white crown. Although he shows less aptitude for elocution than the Egg-headed Cockatoo (extinct), he is, nevertheless, prized for his liberal coo and his habit of nesting with divergent species. He is semi-nocturnal, exhibiting much hors d'oeuvres hunting activity after dusk. His frequently-chang- ing migratory habits puzzle ornithologists who had heretofore assumed that the Potomac was his permanent nesting ground. The Broadtail is often observed seeking out an empty rostrum before laying an egg. In centuries past, parrots were often seen in the company of swashbuckling buccaneers, but with today's changing modes of piracy, they are limited to premiers, prime ministers and presidents.

OPEN SEASON
On Mavericks, Doves,
Redwings and Pinkos.
Harry S. Truman

Common Boar

(*pontificus maximus*)

The Common Boar (or Slow Lerner as he is sometimes called) can be recognized by his short stature, unkempt appearance, and his small but sensitive snout, which enables him to tell exactly which way the wind is blowing. He is also known for swimming along with the tide, which may account for the fact that he once jumped headlong into the Bay of Pigs. Psychoanalytic naturalists attribute this behavior to intense Castro-ation anxiety. Although not a hunter by disposition, this pig once joined with lower species to prey upon the Horned-Rimmed Rosenberg (*vita extincta*).

Pontificus is in great demand for cocktail parties, television panels, and Hadassah gatherings due to his ability to deal with the insignificant in a profound and condescending manner. While boars are quite common in the academic community, this one must feed alone at the academic trough due to his malodorous position on Vietnam. The young boar is colored with distinctive Marx, but the mature animal would rather be fed than red.

The Varying Hare
[*Kennedyctyl vascillayti*]

The Varying Hare can backtrack with such speed and agility that to the untrained eye it appears that there are two hares running in opposite directions. In this respect he reminds one of the Jack Rabbit, to whom he bears a strong resemblance. Mother Nature, in her finite wisdom, has endowed the Varying Hare with the ability to change color with differing climatic conditions. Hence his name. Recent hops to the plains of Africa and the jungles of Harlem, for example, have turned him a militant pink, and he thumps loudly for civil rights. Naturalists, however, recall that when burrowed in the Cabinet, he saw to it that empty perches in Southern courthouses were filled with White Nuthatches. Once fond of nibbling in Farmer McCarthy's cabbage patch, the Varying Hare has long since deserted for more fashionable crops. His breeding habits are nothing short of phenomenal.

The Wahoo

[*Thespis Californicus*]

The Wahoo is easily recognized by his smooth, scaleless skin, his slippery utterances and his chestnut-colored head (which never grays). In previous seasons, the Wahoo laid his eggs on the Warner Brothers' estuary but he now swims up and down the California coast in a noble attempt to make the world safe for hypocracy. Although his philosophy is blubbery and his rhetoric inedible, he is of great commercial value to many industries which profit from his toothy smile and oily pitch.

The Lumpfish

[*Politico Californicus*]

The Lumpfish (or California Weakfish as it is sometimes called) is distinguished by his completely undistinguished appearance. He enjoys mouthing platitudes about capital punishment, decent living standards and freedom of speech, but his weak backbone keeps him from acting upon them. In spite of this he is considered a good catch by union officials who are terribly concerned lest he become extinct. When not drifting along with the prevailing currents, he enjoys floundering in a sea of expediency.

LET US NOW PRAISE EPONYMOUS MEN

Illustrations from WORD PEOPLE, a collection of biographical sketches of persons who lent their names to the English language, by Nancy Caldwell Sorel. Courtesy of American Heritage Press.

George M. Pullman

Samuel Agustus Maverick

63

Nicolas Chauvin

Earl of Cardigan

Luigi Galvani

64

James Watt

Earl of Sandwich

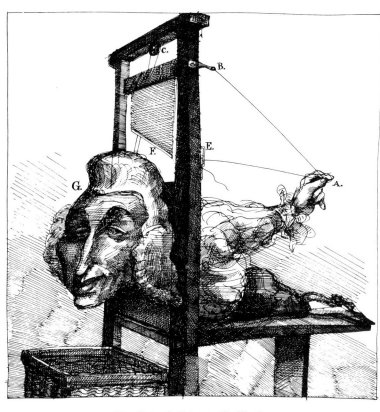

Dr. Joseph Ignace Guillotin

Ambrose E. Burnside

Samuel Plimsoll

"Teddy" Roosevelt

66

Dr. Franz Anton Mesmer

Marquis de Sade

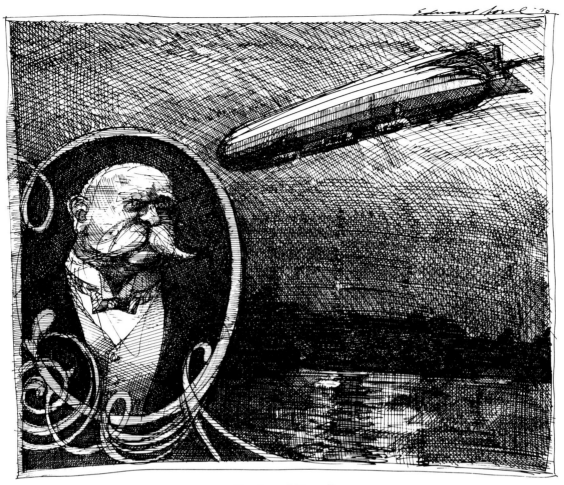

Ferdinand Zeppelin

Rudolph Diesel

Henry Havelock

Unfamiliar Quotations

From the series that appeared in *Atlantic* in 1968.

I was only following marauders.

Truth is booty. Booty is truth.

Every clod has a silver lining.

To hare is human.

A public office is a public lust.

We pry harder.

See what the·goys in the back room will have.

The medium has a message.

The theory of the seizure class.

Mia culpa.

*My·only regret is that I have but
one country to give for my life.*

On a clear day I can see forever.

Following Orders

A miscellany of art done on assignment

Columbia Records, 1971

FROM EACH ACCORDING
TO HIS ABILITY...
TO EACH ACCORDING
TO HIS GREED

John Lewinsay

72

Ney Chasse les Marchands du Temple

SANE, 1970

From the people who brought you Vietnam:

The anti ballistic missile system.

73

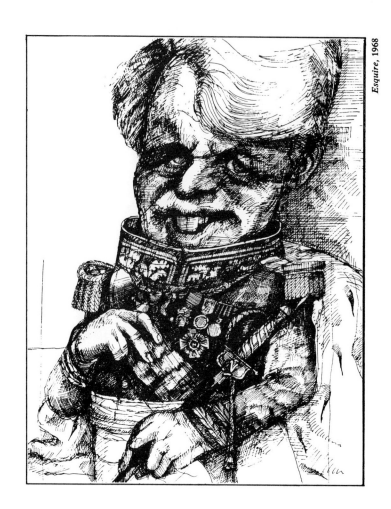

74

Esquire, 1968

76 Schubert

Wagner

Acoustic Research, 1969

Handel

Mozart

LOS ANGELES TIMES DECEMBER 12, 1971

west

Presenting:
Kid Tunney
and His
Balancing Act

Harris Poll

LUP POLL

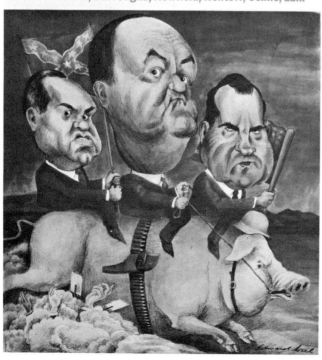

THE
RICHARD M. NIXON
LIBRARY
Some modest proposals

Death follows life. Winter follows fall. Libraries follow Presidents. Richard M. Nixon will have his library just as his predecessors have had theirs. It is foolish to argue with the inevitable, and the city council of Whittier, California, would be the last to try. For it is in Whittier that past, present, and future Nixonia is slated to reside. City Manager N. Keith Abbott has found the "perfect site"—a hillside plot near Whittier College, Mr. Nixon's alma mater—and he has authorized several architects to prepare drawings to show the President.

Now, before these plans go any further, before any more architects are called in, before friends of the President start putting the touch on West Coast fat cats to "start the ball rolling," before the bulldozers show up, I should like to make one thing perfectly clear: Whittier is not the place to build the Nixon Library.

More to the point, California is not the right state. It was, after all, the scene of Nixon's most humiliating defeat. Now, can anyone, after the events of 1962, suggest that any town in California is "the perfect site"? Would it not be more fitting to build this edifice in an area where our President has triumphed? Placing the Nixon Library in California is about as appropriate as placing Napoleon's tomb near Waterloo or the Johnson Library in Woodstock.

One alternative to Whittier is Bay Biscayne. Floridians have always been strong supporters of the President, and the Elysian climate there is certain to attract many visitors to a repository of Nixonia. Bebe Rebozo, a native of that area and a close friend of the President's, is reported to be very keen on having the library there. Rumor has it that he has, in fact, already spoken to the Presi-

dent about the possibility of building the library as the central feature of an enclosed, air-conditioned shopping mall.

But the logical site for the Nixon Library is neither Whittier nor Bay Biscayne. It is Wall Street.

79

THE RICHARD M. NIXON LIBRARY AND MISSILE SITE

Since any edifice dedicated to Mr. Nixon would be a prime target for an enemy attack, it must be protected. The Library itself will be unique on two counts: (1) it will be run by a private corporation with authority to franchise other Nixon Libraries throughout the country; (2) it will be made entirely of plastic.

This article originally appeared in *Atlantic* magazine.

It was to Wall Street that Mr. Nixon came after his shattering defeat of 1962, and it was there that he recovered his physical and emotional health. There, mid the canyons of cold steel and glass, locked into Musaked elevators and whisked away in dark, impersonal limousines, the plucky Californian worked hard and long under flickering fluorescents until he had achieved those legal and financial victories that were to prepare him for the presidency. On Wall Street the Nixon Library would become, like the Statue of Liberty, a landmark that the foreign visitor or returning American could look for as he sailed into New York Harbor.

As for the library itself, it should be—or should strive to be—that which so few presidential libraries are: a true and honest reflection of the man it celebrates. For this reason I suggest that the entire building and management of the library be turned over to the private sector. There is no reason why the Nixon Library should not realize a healthy profit. The time has come for presidential libraries to drop their tax-deductible status, pull themselves up by their own bootstraps, and take their rightful place in the free-enterprise community of man.

My plans for the Nixon Library attempt to do just that. I respectfully submit them for the President's consideration.

THE OATH OF ENTRANCE
Although we all believe that intelligent, nonviolent dissent is healthy in a democracy, we must nevertheless protect the Library against vandalism from radical-liberals. I therefore suggest that all visitors be required to affirm their loyalty to God and country before purchasing tickets. If possible, admission should be kept within the President's price guidelines. Corporation executives, with or without their parents, will be admitted at half price.

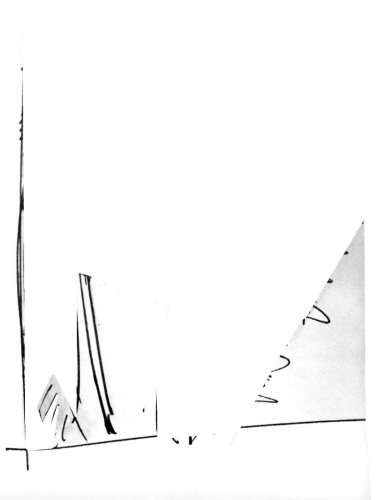

THE MAIN HALL

*Reflecting Mr. Nixon's concern with "the little fellow,"
the Library will greet all visitors with a salute of
crossed swords from the Library's guards. Their
uniforms, of course, will be designed by the President himself.*

FRIENDSHIP PATIO

Overlooking an accurate replica of the Burning Tree golf course, with the New York skyline in the distance, Friendship Patio offers Library visitors a moment of quiet reflection. Patterned after ancient Roman terraces, it will pay homage to President Nixon's distinguished friends, with marble busts of Jackie Gleason, Billy Graham, Murray Chotiner, Bob Hope, and Bebe Rebozo.

MEMORABILIA

In the East Wing visitors will thrill to the sight of the Nixons' first color television set, the last collar and leash worn by Checkers, Mrs. Nixon's famous cloth coat, Tricia's bronzed first shoes, a plastic replica of the pumpkin that figured in the Hiss case, and some of the eighty-two American Legion caps worn by Mr. Nixon during the 1968 campaign.

READING ROOM

Display cases in the West Wing will house letters from Premier Papadopoulos, President Thieu, Vice President Ky, Generalissimo Franco, President Duvalier, President Chiang Kai-shek, and other leaders of the free world.

THE HALL OF FREE ENTERPRISE

This charming promenade, near the Annenberg Gardens, serves as a reminder of President Nixon's unswerving faith in our economic system and his imaginative program to promote "Black Capitalism." Here one will find courteous and charming Afro-Americans who, with the aid of federal funds, have set up their own businesses.

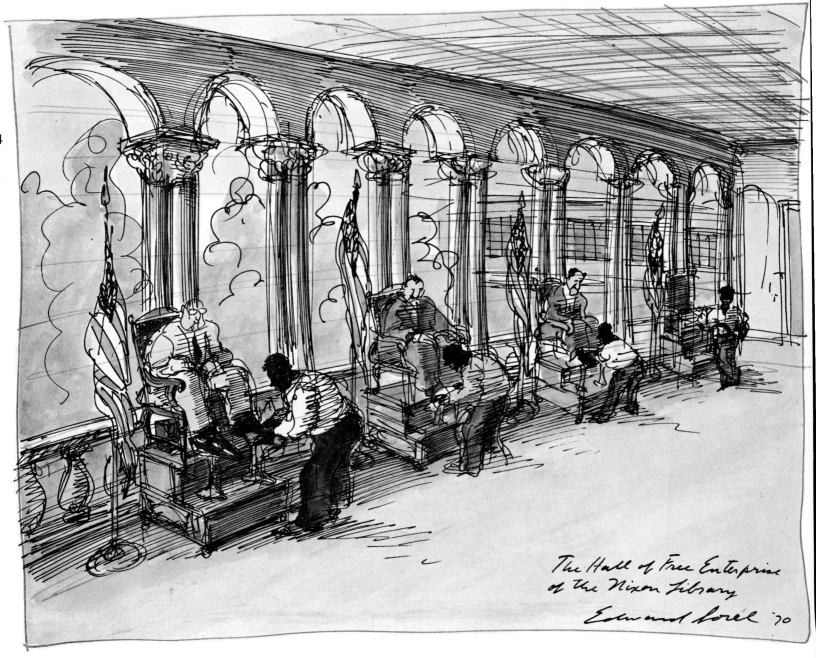

The Hall of Free Enterprise of the Nixon Library

Edward Sorel '70

85

THE ANNENBERG GARDENS

North of the Library is an ideal setting for promenades and statues. The allegorical sculpture above depicts the President removing his Wall Street homburg and donning his war helmet in preparation for his inauguration.

ROCKEFELLER HALL

The Library's auditorium, generously donated by New York's governor, will have regular showings of Patton, Chisum, The Sound of Music, *and other favorites of the President. The film library will be under the supervision of Miss Tricia Nixon, and there will be no showings of movies with an X, R, or GP rating.*

THE PRESIDENT'S VAULT

Visitors will certainly want to visit the maximum security vault on the ground floor. The giant safe, designed especially for the library by Krupp, holds the secret details of President Nixon's plans for ending the war in Vietnam and winning the peace, controlling inflation, and bringing us together. The President has donated these documents to the Library with the understanding that they will not be available to the public until 1992.

MEMENTOS

Before leaving, the entire family is certain to want a souvenir. For their convenience gift shops are located near each exit. Mother may purchase a Pat 'n' Dick© carving set or a David 'n' Julie© ashtray, while Junior will want one of the books from the President Nixon Self-Help Library©. Dad is sure to cherish one of the handsome busts of our President. They're ideal for office or den and made of genuine plaster de Paris.

86

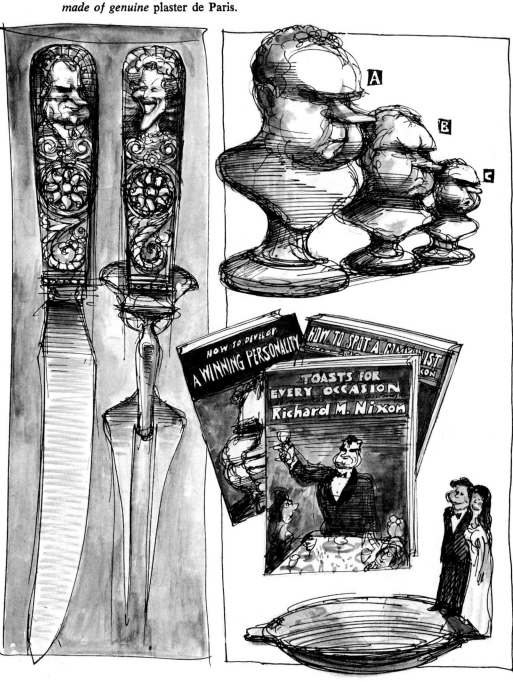

In case you don't recognize everyone, here's a Who's Who of those not named in the text

In Glorious Living Color
Roger Vadim, Jane Fonda, Henry Fonda, Svetlana Alliluyeva, Jacqueline Onassis,
Francis Cardinal Spellman, Terrence Cardinal Cooke, (Famous Writers School) William
Shakespeare, Oscar Wilde, Samuel Johnson, Gertrude Stein, Ernest Hemingway, Voltaire,
Mark Twain, Leo Tolstoy, Edgar Allan Poe, Dylan Thomas, Senator Jacob Javits.

Beastiary
Arthur Goldberg, Max Lerner, Robert Kennedy, Timothy O'Leary,
Ronald Reagan, Pat Brown.

Unfamiliar Quotations
Moisha Dyan, Ayn Rand, Norman Vincent Peale, Hugh Hefner, Richard Nixon,
J. Edgar Hoover, Norman Podhoretz, Bishop James Pike, Dean Rusk, Frank Sinatra,
General Nguyen Cao Ky, John Kenneth Galbraith.

Following Orders
Richard Ney.